LIVING THE COMMANDMENTS

by

William Lawson, SJ

CATHOLIC TRUTH SOCIETY

PUBLISHERS TO THE HOLY SEE

CONTENTS

WHY COMMANDMENTS?

A measure of human behaviour that has been used throughout Old Testament and New Testament times is the Ten Commandments. They appear in the catechisms, with explanations of what they prescribe and what they forbid. The older catechisms make more of prohibition than of precept; yet even when that false emphasis is changed the Ten Commandments are not a sufficient guide to the Christian way of life. Except for the third, and the preamble of the first, they are natural law, and have of themselves nothing to do with supernatural life. Besides, eight of them are negatives. They are not, by themselves, the law by which the Jews lived. When our Lord was asked by a lawyer which was the great Commandment of the law, he gave two: the love of God and the love of neighbour, both from the Old Testament (Deut 6:5 and Lev 19:18). Those two Commandments are the essentials of Christian living. As St Paul says: 'You shall not commit adultery, you shall not kill, you shall not steal, you shall not covet, and so on, are summed up in this single command: You must love your neighbour as yourself. Love is the one thing that cannot hurt your neighbour; that is why it is the answer to every one of the Commandments.'

All the same, the Ten Commandments are recommended as headings for research into Christian behaviour: they come from God, and are warnings about particular evil tendencies in human nature; and they are traditional and known to everybody.

Why Commandments at all? It is a question to be answered, because it is implied in the grievance that so many people feel at restraint in their liberty. Rules for conduct are resented, and then their authority is questioned. Why must we go to Mass on Sundays; why can't there be divorce when marriage has obviously broken down beyond repair; what authority can come between two people who love one another?

There is not a single entity in the whole of the universe that doesn't live under Commandments: and the Commandments are, so to say, built in – they are a statement of what the entity is, its nature, construction and function. The pig, for example, lives under the command 'You shall not fly' – because it is not built for flying. Heavenly bodies keep to the courses determined for them by their constitution and position: and they are so law-abiding that astronomers can predict their movements centuries ahead. We ourselves expect the lesser creation to observe the laws of their being – the sun and moon must appear at the right times, a lamb must not become a ravening beast of prey, apple trees must produce apples and not plums or nylon socks. Without order, life would be chaotic, unpredictable – in short, unlivable. Order depends on every creature being what it was made to be, keeping the law of its nature. St Augustine says: 'The will of the sublime Creator makes itself known in the nature of every created being. According to God's law, the poles of heaven turn and the stars follow their course, the sun lights up the day and the moon the night, and the great universe keeps its order through days, months, years, sun-years, and star-years, in the steady change of the season'. (The City of God, 21.8).

A human being is of a certain kind, with certain built-in rules of conduct. God's will is that human beings should keep these rules of conduct and so be the kind of creature that he made them.

It is unreasonable in a human being either to resent the rules which are part of his being or to make different rules. The only rules on which we will work are the ones implied in our nature. We don't say: 'I'll run my car on water instead of petrol'. We don't say: 'I'll step out of the plane when it is over my house, and save the tedious drive from the airport'. The car isn't made that way; we aren't made that way physically. Personally we are not made for atheism, adultery, murder, lying and theft: and they are as damaging to the person as drinking poison would be to the body. We should be delighted to know our rules for good living, and recite Psalm 118 with enthusiasm.

When he becomes conscious of himself as designed, the human being must worship the Designer, accepting the design. Acceptance of the design, and all that it implies of steady fulfilment of the design in behaviour, means acceptance of God's will as the permanent standard of right conduct. It also means agreement with God about happiness. Human happiness is the completeness of the person, so that nothing is lacking to him. It is attainable only by being what God meant the human person to be. The attainment of happiness is only by doing the will of God.

Religion begins there, in awe of God as the Creator of the person, and in a personal response to God's implied question: 'Will you be what I made you to be?' The human being answers 'Yes', and continues throughout life a dialogue with God, offering self to God to do His will whenever a decision has to be made.

It can be seen that what is wanted at once and all the time is a habit of prayer. The dialogue with God should become continuous. Religion then will not be a school-life conformity or a chameleon-like anonymity in society, but a deliberate direction of self to God. Its constituents are three: firstly, an awareness or consciousness of God's existence and His concern for me as a person; secondly, a docile or willing-to-learn attention to God, so as to know what He wants me to do; thirdly, a readiness to do His will as soon as it is known.

FAITH, HOPE AND CHARITY

The first three commandments are about man's direct relations with the Family of the Blessed Trinity. They call on man to take God seriously. The supreme reality is God: the supreme reality in any human life should be God – not just in theory, as though God were one of the astonishing facts, like the height of Everest, that can be preserved in a reference book and forgotten by man. Taking God seriously is directing oneself to Him determinedly and continuously with the powers of mind and will called faith, hope and charity. They are all very hard work; but they all make an incomparable contribution to the person who exercises them. Any virtue is its own reward in the sense that it is an employment of self which makes the self more real: virtue in action is self-realisation. These three virtues are the greatest in their object and in the concentration of human forces which they require. Human personality grows more out of the exercise of faith, hope and charity than out of any other exercise: and without them human personality is stunted. They are not then just names, to be rattled off in catechism answers, or static possessions like Christening mugs: they are powers in the Christian mind and will, which should be in continuous use.

Faith, natural and universal, is knowledge accepted on authority and then the use or assertion of that knowledge. Everybody uses other people's knowledge. 'If you want to know the time, ask a policeman'. We take the word of public servants, newspapers, radio and television, teachers and all kinds of specialists. Divine faith is firstly an acceptance of the authority of God, then the possession of the truths made known by God, and then the assertion of those truths in one's whole way of living.

There should be a keen gratitude for the gift of faith. In ordinary life, how comforting it is to know – to know your job, the way about, your own language, the time, all sorts of truth! How satisfying it would be to know all about astronomy, nuclear fission, industry and commerce, history, philosophy… But the greatest extent and depth of natural knowledge is nothing to the riches of truth possessed by faith: and the authority for these truths is entirely trustworthy. Here is truth of immeasurable value possessed with perfect assurance.

The first duty in such possession is to start examining the truths. Again, they are not a string of words, as in a gabbled Creed: they are the facts to be known and acted on so as to live realistically. They are even less circumscribed than natural truth. Nobody in his senses would ever close his books and his mind, saying: 'There! I know all about carpentry, English, arithmetic, medicine'… Still less would it make sense to say: 'I know all about my religion'. And whereas we can say about particular subjects, 'That's enough mathematics for my purposes', we can never reasonably put a limit to our knowledge of the content of faith. There is a permanent obligation to be always learning. The most important way is prayer – a deliberate presence to God, docility in His presence, and readiness to do His will. Christians with a habit of reading should always have a book or two going which bear on the truths of faith. Why not read the Bible? (It is revealing that when this suggestion is made to any fairly large representative group of Catholics, a good number of them look astonished, and are obviously rejecting the proposal, as though you had urged them to sail an open boat single-handed across the Atlantic.) There are many books on theology, philosophy, the scriptures, and the history of the Church which are not only instructive and a good background for the habit of prayer, but also very readable. It is worth acquiring a taste for them.

Other reading and study illuminates Christian doctrine. Medicine, botany, biology, astronomy – all the natural sciences - are subjects in their own right, but they all study God's creation. Take astronomy as an example, for its illumination of the idea of immensity and for the salutary cold water it throws on man's overheated claims that he is about to conquer space. A few figures cut man down to size and put him in the mood to recite Psalm 8: 'I look up at your heavens, made by your fingers, at the moon and stars you set in place – ah, what is man that you should spare a thought for him, the son of man that you should care for him?', and Psalm 148: 'Praise the Lord, O sun and moon, praise him all you shining stars'. The sun is 1,390,000 kilometres in diameter: it is a notable star for us, but a mere speck in the universe. The sun's nearest neighbour of importance is Alpha Centauri, 40 billion km. distant. After that, figures become too large to have much meaning, so a unit of distance, a light year, has been adopted for astronomical numbers. It is the distance light travels in a year, 10 billion km. Alpha Centauri is four light years away from the sun. The Milky Way which we look at in the night sky, and of which we and the sun are part, is 100,000 light years long, and between 7,000 and 10,000 light years thick: it contains between 10 million and 200 million stars, all of them, including our sun, moving round the centre of the galaxy at the rate of 300 km. a second: one complete orbit takes 200 million years. The galaxy next to ours is that of Andromeda. It is one and a half million light years away – one and a half million times ten billion kilometres. Both galaxies are specks in the universe. 'When I see the heavens, the work of your hands…'

But knowledge by itself is not the whole of faith. Nor is it enough to acknowledge divine truths as intellectual propositions merely, so that 'I believe in God, creator of heaven and earth', has the same force as 'I believe there is ice at the poles'. Belief in God means acceptance of the truth that He is, that His goodness is unlimited, and we come from Him, depend on Him every moment, exist to do His will, and, with every breath we draw, move nearer to His eternity. The only realistic assertion of the truths of faith is a habit of prayer, a habit, that is to say, of bringing ourselves deliberately into the presence of God, there to do Him reverence and to find out what He wants us to be and how He wants us to act. From that presence – which is God's point of view – we should look at ourselves, our circumstances, the world and its people, and see creation as God sees it, adopting His values for things and human beings: and then, in very decision and action, we should do His will.

The hope that 'springs eternal in the human breast' is not necessarily even a natural virtue. Accepting the fact that their future is largely out of their control, human beings can either hope or despair. They usually hope – that they will pass their exams, marry happily, stay alive, and so on and on. Hope of heaven is not necessarily a virtue either: it could be a belief in life after death together with a commonsense preference for peace and happiness.

A life of hope, on the contrary, is determined and strenuous. It is the deliberate adoption of the purpose in life indicated by God in His creation of man and in all His teaching of man, and the taking of all measures necessary to achieve that purpose, all in co-operation with God and confidence in His providence.

We are accustomed to the relationship between ends and means. If someone announces his intention of being a lawyer we don't take him seriously if he doesn't study. A genuine purpose of going to the United States includes raising the fare, getting a visa, and submitting to injections. It is not a vague expectation of waking up one morning and finding oneself in New York.

Hope is the direction of one's life to God and to permanent presence in His family, and the subordination of all other purposes to that one. The hopeful man is intent on eternal life and therefore necessarily on supernatural life, which is eternal life in its temporal form. Hope looks right across time to the point where it meets eternity: but it sees the intervening years with a practical and selective eye as the period of making certain under God that life has its right conclusion. With the practice of hope goes qualification for the happiness of the Beatitudes: Blessed are they who hunger and thirst for the supernatural life: they shall have their fill. Blessed are they who suffer persecution for the sake of supernatural life, for theirs is the kingdom of heaven. Hope is not wishful thinking or a dull yearning for pie in the sky: it is a firm answer, maintained day by day and honoured in every choice, to God's invitation to belong to His house and family.

Like faith, hope implies a habit of prayer – awareness of God, readiness to know His will and do it. It has a transforming effect on character, because it brings a consciousness of the providence of God, from which spring serenity and courage, and a readiness, in one's own peace, to be a help to others. The discipline of hope is hard: but it is fruitful.

To start at the wrong end about charity: we need it. Without it we can never make a worthwhile job of ourselves. St Peter says: 'Study to present yourselves unto God a workman of whom He need not be ashamed'. The work we bring for God to inspect is not a career, or a dynasty, or a standard of living: it is our own self, the character and personality we have made in our time and space. It is made with charity. Other elements come in: but without charity it will be a botch. We shall be ashamed of ourselves, and God will be ashamed of us.

The reason is that we grow as persons by sharing in the life of other persons. Physically we grow by using the lesser creation – air, food, light. Intellectually we grow by making truth our own, taking it where we find it. Personally we grow by possessing persons – but we possess them not by capture or enslavement or domination, for they belong to themselves, but only by recognising their goodness in themselves and devoting ourselves to them for their sake.

The infinite perfection of personality belongs to the Blessed Trinity. We need Father, Son and Holy Spirit: and only by dedicating ourselves to them can we nourish our being on theirs. The first Commandment of charity, 'You shall love the Lord your God, with your whole mind and heart and soul, and all your strength', is not an extra introduced into human life after it was fully constituted. It is a statement of what a human being is, like saying 'You shall breathe', 'You shall eat', 'You shall think'. Unless we love God we cannot be properly human, and fit for ourselves to live with: we are bound to be grossly defective in personal being.

Charity is so tall an order, and communication with God is so different from human relations, that Christians are inclined to close their minds to it, or to whittle it down until it seems do-able. But it is our Lord's version of it which is right, and of obligation. They had better face the full demand of charity.

In practice, they can't do more than their best: and their best can be very good. In ordinary life, the first endeavour in love is to know the other person. That is what courting and engagement are about. Presence, geographical if possible, and always of mind and heart, is necessary. But that is what Awareness means: and it is obvious and straightforward to add Alertness to God's prompting and Availability for His will. Like faith and hope, but more urgently, charity requires a habit of prayer.

REVERING GOD AND HIS CREATION

You shall not take the name of the Lord your God in vain.

Here's another Commandment that needn't delay us very long. Vows? That's for people with a 'vocation'. Oaths? Jury service, witness box: that's once in a lifetime. Cursing and swearing? 'Damn' doesn't count, and we aren't in a Catholic country, so blasphemy needn't concern us. Next, please.

Read this Commandment in its Old Testament context, and see how much it should mean to us. The 'name' of God is the being of God, the divine nature, and the Blessed Trinity. We should be in awe of God permanently, and have deep reverence for the sacredness of His being. His presence, in which we believe, should be real to us – much more real than the presence of heads of state, or 'personalities' of the entertainment industry, or the boss, or even those we love. We should be sensitive to the holiness of God and conform our lives to that infinite fact: as He Himself teaches us: 'I am the Lord your God. Be holy because I am holy', and 'Be perfect as your heavenly Father is perfect'.

There are people who identify name and personal life. They keep their name secret, because if enemies gained possession of the name they would have power over the person. God has told us His name – He is the Necessary Being. He has revealed Himself to us through the Prophets and, last of all, through the Second Person of the Trinity, and has enabled us in Christ to be His children, members of His family, with a rightful place in His house.

The dialogue with God must be maintained. Our created holiness of supernatural life must answer the deliberate presence to us of His uncreated holiness. We respond with faith, hope and charity, made continuous in a habit of prayer.

We answer as well in our respect for the sacredness of people. Those who have supernatural life share in a human way in the holiness of God; in St Peter's words, they are partakers in the divine nature. They are sacred both individually and in their community with Christ in the Church. We are accustomed to special respect owed to offices in the Church, as of Bishop, or to states, as of religious. There is an underlying and universal respect owed to the whole people of God.

Every day is full of encounters with these people whose sacredness demands our profound respect. We think about them, bump into them, go to visit them, work with them, discuss them with others. We cannot meet our obligations to them except by educating ourselves to a permanent attitude: otherwise we shall be too slow in our response to their reality. That education could be a habit of prayer: along the lines of the three A's. We should train ourselves to be immediately aware of the person's immeasurable value, to be always alert to needs, and to be available to meet them. The essential holiness of God, and the conferred holiness of His people, should be respected in one and the same direction of our lives.

Remember to keep holy the Sabbath day

Catholics would have their own population-problem if all who could went to Mass on Sundays and holy days of obligation. Their problem at present is different – that of Catholics who don't go to Mass. Most of them used to go, and their failure to go now raises the question why they went at all. Most of them would still be regular in their attendance at Mass if their presence before was part of their faith, hope and charity, and of their habit of prayer: and for a resumed attendance the requirement would be a renewal of faith, hope and charity, and prayer. It is useless to urge obedience to the Church on those who are unwilling to accept her authority, or to recall the facts of heaven and hell to those whose faith is at most nominal. There will continue to be droves of non-practising Catholics so long as upbringing fails to establish them in faith, hope, charity and prayer which will demand community worship of God.

The sacrifice of the Mass being the perfect worship of God, Christians should spontaneously take part in it, and should welcome the third Commandment which brings them all together once a week for a satisfying duty. For them, Mass attendance is not a solitary event alien to the main business of life, to the serious occupations of qualifying for a career, holding down a job, providing for dependants, pursuing hobbies and enjoying leisure: it is the highlight of life's main business, which is to be in God's presence and do His will.

The third Commandment is positive in form, but it becomes as much a burden as prohibitions unless it is welcomed. Sunday Mass will be no more than a duty, neglected, or begrudgingly done under threat, if it is not presented in the framework of faith, hope and charity, the redemption and the attainment of personal perfection. Desire to worship God in the Mass comes from a Christian way of living, and not from a command, however strongly and frequently uttered.

But when faith, hope and charity, and prayer, make community worship desirable, real community worship should be possible. The Mass is the perfect sacrifice, the perfect worship of God. But the desire of willing worshippers is not met unless they can take their part in the sacrifice which is their offering with Christ.

At this point, an examination of conscience could be profitable. In the Church, the essentials are preserved unchanged but the non-essentials alter. The full revelation of Christ is in the care of the Church, and it has been thought about and meditated on for centuries, so that its content and meaning have become steadily clearer. We have the same sacrifice as the first generation of Christians, but its outward circumstances have altered to suit the needs of different generations.

Because we conserve so much as divinely appointed conservators, we tend to be conservative even when we ought to change. Church architecture and music, clerical dress, religious instruction in schools and pulpits, 'devotions', religious vocabulary – they have all changed. The changes, however, are haphazard, slower than they need be, and hampered by a cult of the archaic – preference for what is because it has always been so. But externals and accidentals – music, architecture, ecclesiastical and religious dress, the language of hymns, teaching methods, and the style and contents of sermons – exist not in their own right but as means to ends. They all need revision from time to time, to make sure that they are doing their job.

The externals of the liturgy are a means to an end. Do they allow and invite the right degree and manner of participation in the Mass? What are the right degree and manner? Dialogue Mass, large use of the vernacular, Mass facing the people, the Canon said aloud…? God's people have not only a right to an opinion but a duty to form one, to the best of their ability, by studying the modern liturgical movement and taking as helpful a part in it as they can. Bishops will decide the practice in their diocese, but their decisions take account of public opinion.

When is all this reading to be done? Anyone who wants to read can make half an hour a day for it, perhaps by eschewing the kind of print which is mostly used to kill time – magazines and evening papers. On Sunday, the day of rest, there is rather more leisure which could be used for steady reading – of liturgy at need, but in general of what comes under the heading of the Word of God. A Sunday instruction in church and the reading of the Epistle and Gospel of the Mass could be supplemented by Teach Yourself application. It is irresponsible for Catholics to cease studying their religion when they leave school or college or university. They have their share in 'the ministry of the Word'. They may be, for some enquirers, the only source of news – the Good News or Gospel of Christianity. The least they can do is to know the substance of the news and be able to pass it on. Incompetence in that God-given task is shameful.

Honour your Father and your Mother

The first three Commandments are about the Blessed Trinity, and our knowledge, love and service of God the Father, God the Son, and God the Holy Spirit.

The rest of the Commandments come under the second law of charity, 'You shall love your neighbour as yourself'.

To keep that Commandment we must know how we love ourselves. I love myself not emotionally or passionately, but matter-of-factly, by putting a value on myself. To me I am the most important person in the world, whose success in life simply must be achieved. I am in never-ending possession of my personal version of human nature, having one stretch of time in which to qualify for eternal happiness, and holding a passport from God who started me on my journey and awaits me at the end of it. I have a title to everybody's esteem and help, not because I am this or that but just because I am.

That being the way I regard myself, it is the way I must regard others.

To the lawyer's question, 'Who is my neighbour?' Our Lord answered with the parable of the Good Samaritan, from which it appears that our neighbour is anyone who needs our help. That means everybody. Every person we ever meet will need at least our respect, kindness, understanding, interest. We must develop perceptiveness or sensitivity, a sort of Christian power of diagnosis. We know our own needs: we must know the needs of others.

Awareness and alertness should lead to effective service. In His description of the Last Judgment, Our Lord admits to His Kingdom those only who have done the works of mercy. To crown consciousness of the value and needs of others, we must serve them at least as well as we serve ourselves.

The programme of charity there summarised is life-long and world-wide. Its immensity in time and space need not deter Christians from embarking on it. As the fourth Commandment says, it starts at home.

In charity, as in living, we work outwards from a centre, dealing with one after another of a series of concentric circles.

In both life and charity we begin at home, and that is reason enough for the appearance of 'Honour your Father and your Mother' amongst the Commandments. Parents, brothers and sisters are persons of immeasurable value and endless needs. The ties of blood and association, and particular debts to parents, should give love a special delicacy and durability. Unfortunately, the warning of the Commandment is often needed. Members of families can allow familiarity to blunt awareness, so that they treat other members of the family as household fixtures or moving furniture. At their place of work they are bright, courteous and communicative: at home they are dull, rude and monosyllabic. They ought, once a week or so, to call a mental roll of their family, and say, after each name, 'My Father (or Mother, or Sister, or Brother), who is also a person'.

Mention of the Father and Mother reminds us that the generations tend to be uneasy with one another. Prejudices are bound to exist, but in charity we should be able to turn them to good account. The world of study, games, entertainment, careers and threats of war which the young have to cope with hasn't existed before. The similar world their parents faced is ancient history to the children: and the children's age is the parents' middle age. Parents aren't with it any more, and they are solidly square.

O.K. Persons come in all shapes, and charity must come, too, from both sides.

Home is family to start with. It extends. Young and old have friends: they belong to communities: their circles increase in number, and inside each one the same charity should operate.

The word which best sums up this work of charity is participation. Awareness of the value of each person in a community such as an office or school or workshop or college begins with acknowledgement that the persons exist. It is a basic Christian exercise to know their faces and names, so that they may be reached with greetings and other courtesies. After that, the more life can be shared, the better. Gospel exhortations to Christians to be leaven in the mass or light in the darkness, and Pius XII's appeal to them to transform their society, show the necessity of living and working with others. Some solitude is necessary for anyone, but it is not family life to be always withdrawn, living to oneself. Christians cannot have a Christianising effect on schools, colleges, universities, factories, offices, local, national and international affairs if they live to themselves either individually or in groups.

Home also means hospitality. To be welcoming in heart and features, and practically, is a good human and Christian characteristic. It is necessary at any time for the perfection of Christian personality: it is especially needed in these days of displaced persons, refugees, colour bar, United Nations and United Europe. The tendency to maintain a succession of prejudices from adolescence to old age, so constricting to mind and heart, should be overcome by charity which is aware, alert and available.

CHARITY AND CHASTITY

You shall not kill

It is a waste of breath to shout 'You shall not kill' at gunmen whose livelihood is murder, or at abortionists who take the life of the unborn from the highest motives, or at ruthless drivers who think they are skilled enough to beat all hazards. What is needed is a Christian conviction of the sanctity of human life which will show itself everywhere in all possible ways. The Christian asserts his right not only to life but to a full life. Loving his neighbour as himself, he must work to secure a full life for everyone.

How many of the millions of deaths every year are preventable? They should all be on the Christian conscience – and they are quite a burden. Many millions of legal and illegal abortions yearly: more millions of deaths from famine, under-nourishment and disease; traffic deaths by the tens of thousands; and, in addition, lives grossly impaired by poverty, hunger and disease, hopelessly painful through lack of necessaries such as decent dwelling-places, honourable work, a minimum of security, or the beginnings of opportunity for self-realisation.

It is easy for Christians to fall into the 'I'm, all right Jack' frame of mind. They don't have to minister to the dying and bury the dead, try to check and root out disease, give hope and courage to the despairing. Their conscience can be soothed with the thought that 'they' will do what is necessary – the government, UNO, the Church, the professional healers and helpers: and with a quiet conscience they can enjoy life, make a career, settle down to comfort and security. But it is personal response which is enquired into by Our Lord when He mentions hunger and thirst to each one at the Judgment.

Again, what is first wanted is awareness – knowledge of the numbers of human beings doomed to untimely death or denied a full life, and consciousness of each one as a person with all the human rights and an eternal destiny. That awareness includes respect and compassion. They are already better off because we pray for them as our own. Alertness leads to a study of ways and means – study at one's own level, which may be no more than finding out what organisation to support, what measure of government help to press for, or what ideals of self-sacrifice to practise in almsgiving. Availability means anything from intelligent votes in local and national government, to devoted service in a profession such as nursing, teaching or medicine, to committee work for welfare organisations, to a year or two spent in an under-developed country sharing life with the people and passing on skills to them, to the lifelong support given in the background by the mother of a family.

Using life under the providence of God means making the most of talents. There is a natural inclination to do that. But it is more than natural to plan life for the benefit of others. Without instruction and prompting, young Christians might think exclusively of career, success, security and a firmly established way of life, or, with a shorter view, of pocket-money and independence. They ought to know that, whether or not they have a 'vocation' in the limited sense, they certainly have a vocation to charity. They are called as Christians to a life of charity: their personal worth depends on the exercise of charity: they are examined in charity at the end of their time. According to their talents they should choose their life's work and status for its content of charity. There are some jobs which are in themselves works of mercy: and there is no honourable job which cannot be done for love of God and of God's people.

You shall not covet your neighbour's wife
You shall not commit adultery

If there is one place more than another where the teaching of Christian behaviour is negative, it is under the heading of these two Commandments. An instruction on them was once given in these few words: 'Sixth and ninth Commandments? That's simple. You mustn't and you mustn't want to'. There are good catechisms teaching positive doctrine which seem unable to find a positive for this subject. Unchastity and impurity are wrong. What is right? Obviously chastity and purity. What is chastity? Not being unchaste. What is purity? Not being impure. And we are back to negatives.

That is a great loss of wholesome doctrine, and a grave deprivation for struggling human beings who are not strengthened and inspired by 'You mustn't, and you mustn't want to'.

Yet these Commandments, which seem to be particularly negative, are in fact particularly positive. They are especially Commandments of charity.

There is firstly the love of God. For love of God the human being accepts his nature and keeps it as God made it, using it or not using it – speech, sight, reproductive powers, alimentary system – according to the will of God, making a perfection or near-perfection that he can present to God.

There is then love of human beings, one's neighbour.

A human being ought to be in relationship with his fellows. Without them he can never realise himself (make himself real) and arrive at the perfection of his personality. Like all his relationships, it has to be true to himself and his object. With any being less than human, his attitude is one of getting. He makes things his own by taking and assimilating them. But human beings by definition are self-possessing: they belong to themselves. An approach to a human being to capture or possess or use is false to his nature and makes the relationship wrong. Moreover, a Christian gives to another the value he gives to himself, and treats him therefore as a goodness to be cared for and fostered. He must go out to others, but he must not come back upon himself, as he does with things. His attitude is not one of getting, grasping, using, but of giving.

He gives himself: and not any old self but his best. That makes all human relationships sexual (it is a diabolical confusion to make 'sexual relationship' mean only the physical union of the sexes, and thus put a false emphasis into circulation). The person entering into relationship is man or woman, boy or girl, with the physical, spiritual and personal qualities that belong to sex.

All relationships should be of that self-dedicating kind. It is a gross evil to use another person as though he were a thing or a vegetable or an animal. Human beings are not for use. The fact that they are of the one sex or the other does not alter the truth that they are not for use. The bond between two people should be charity, and their sex is part of the perfection with which they are devoted to the other.

When the relationship is between man and woman, another element can enter. Neither man nor woman is the unit of the human race: the unit is man-and-woman. Each needs the other, and they are naturally drawn to unite. The usual stimulus to effect the union is sexual passion, the physical core of the state known as 'being in love'. By itself that passion is selfish: it is a desire for the satisfaction of the self in the use of the reproductive faculty. It has overtones of varied pleasantness, many of them unselfish: but the root of it is a desire to get or to have.

If there is no other bond between man and woman, the satisfaction of desire brings a certain selfish fulfilment which sooner or later destroys the bond itself – passion is not lasting – and both personalities are diminished by a union inadequate to the deepest needs of their nature.

Ideally, what should happen is this: there is a double bond of charity between a man and a woman: each is dedicated to the other. 'Being in love' gives them a powerful enthusiastic willingness for a particular self-dedication. The man will belong to the woman for her fulfilment in womanhood as wife and mother: the woman will belong to the man for his fulfilment in manhood as husband and father. The two self-dedications together form the creative union of marriage.

The principle exemplified in that statement about marriage is that a relationship is right when it preserves and increases the other's self-possession: it is wrong when it damages or diminishes that self-possession. In the ideal marriage each is dedicated to the other for the other's sake, and their relationship increases the self-possession of both.

Perhaps it is boys particularly who need to educate themselves to this principle. Girls are by nature inclined to devote themselves in love. Their passions are less selfish in that they are naturally inseparable from a desire for children. What they seek in a partner is something like the awareness, alertness and availability which are the marks of true love. A boy's passions are more easily aroused, and are more towards getting than giving. They can easily impel towards behaviour which treats the girl as less than a person. However, the fact is wrapped up in 'romance', a girl is used for selfish satisfaction: and to subject another person to use is a wicked denial of charity. She should never be dispossessed by greedy kisses ('French', for example), straying hands and embraces out of control. All show of affection should say, in effect: 'There you are. You belong to yourself'. After any stage in the relationship, the girl should be more self-possessed than before, her personal life fostered by care, delicacy, understanding and support.

The Church's judgment against contraception is a condemnation of a gross misuse of nature – the frustration of the generative purpose of the generative faculty. It is also a defence of the dignity of the person and of personal self-possession, and a demand for deep respect for the person. Contraceptive acts subject a person to use for the selfish satisfaction of the user: and that is a grave offence against charity. If the act is by the will of both partners, the damage to charity is doubled.

Charity supplies the highest motive for behaviour. In boy-girl and man-woman relationships where chastity is in question, it has the great advantage of being able to attract 'love' to its side and to make an ally of the very force which threatens damage. As St Paul has it: 'Love is the one thing that cannot hurt your neighbour' (Rom.13:10).

CHRISTIAN STANDARDS OF LIVING AND TRUTH

You shall not steal
You shall not covet your neighbour's goods

The Christian standard of living is the best there is, the most sensible and the happiest of all. But it takes some learning, as does the meaning of happiness.

Happiness is self-possession, the reality of one's own immortal being, personal completeness. What makes unhappiness is the absence of anything which belongs to one's nature and personality as God intended them to be. Nobody in this life is physically, mentally and personally (in character, personality) complete. There is always something lacking to perfection.

The whole person, not just body and spirit alone, is important for happiness. It is the perfection of the person, moral perfection, which is decisive. A material and a cultural standard of living have their importance, but the moral standard of living is what makes or marrs happiness – what the person is in self, in character, in faith, hope and, above all, charity.

What we know of divine values confirms that judgment. Love of God and love of people are what God looks for in a human being: it is they which give a human being value in self and before God: they make him what he ought to be and ensure his happiness.

All else, then, is relative to character and personality. Material goods should be desirable only as they contribute to personal worth. They have no endless unchanging value in themselves. The right Christian attitude to them is, therefore, one of superiority. The Christian withholds himself calmly while he makes up his mind whether material possessions are going to improve his personal being or not. He rejects them or accepts them according to the measurement. As a result he gains in self-possession. His worth in his own eyes does not depend on externals: he is still himself whether in prosperity or poverty. He is satisfied if others take him as he is in himself, and he can disregard judgments favourable or unfavourable based on the extent of his material possessions.

In his approach to others he has the same standard. The value he is aware of is a personal value, independent of externals. He communicates with the person, and the relationships he establishes have the permanence of personality.

That standard of living cannot be adopted out of hand. It is the fruit of a habit of prayer, of deep, faith, hope and charity, of courage in having a mind of one's own. The great weight of public opinion is against the Christian set

of values, and Christians are in spite of themselves affect-
ed by public opinion.St James had to reprove some of the
early Christians who were all over the rich and neglected
the poor. St Paul wrote to the Hebrews: 'Let your heart be
free from greed for gold: and be content with what you
have' (Heb.13:5). Modern Christians will have to work
hard to reach contentment. They are mostly in the race to
catch up with the one further ahead towards affluence, or
at least not to fall behind the neighbours. Keeping up with
the Joneses is a universal social exercise. There are status
symbols which are sought not for intrinsic value but
because they bring public esteem – in the U.S.A., two
cars, and now two houses; in England, schools, postal
addresses, badges on blazers and labels on luggage,
accents ('when an Englishman opens his mouth he makes
other Englishmen despise him' – My Fair Lady), and
dress. All that is trivial and pitiable: it is also serious
because it means loss of independence of mind, of the
right sort of originality, and of Christian standards in
business and family life. To take only one example: when
husband and wife 'plan' their family (with no contraceptive selfishness and depersonalisation) what considera-
tions weigh with them – faith, hope and charity, the way
their family group will look in eternal life; or house, car,
school, contacts, entertaining, holidays, status symbols
generally, acquaintance with the mammon of iniquity?
Our Lord's example is not for imitation in detail, but we

need His Spirit. He was born in a stable and buried in a borrowed tomb: He had no pillow for His head and not always enough food. He taught us that happiness belongs to those who sit lightly to material possessions.

He also taught us that the poor are always with us and are our responsibility. We must feed the hungry and harbour the homeless. What we have in excess should be given away, and sometimes we could imitate the widow and give away what we really need. 'If a man who was rich enough in this world's goods saw that one of his brothers was in need, but closed his heart to him, how could the love of God be living in him?' (1 Jn 3:17). It is a healthy practice always to be giving away something good from our possessions. 'If you have much, give more; if you have little, give less' (Tob 4:9). To read what Old Testament and New Testament have to say about almsgiving would administer a wholesome shock.

Today we have to bear in mind the extent of our responsibility. In recent years we have found ourselves answerable for all the social injustices in our country. Now, as *Mater et Magistra* tells us, the world has shrunk through ease of communication to the size of a small country. Our 'brother in need' is not just in the next street or claiming unemployment pay in England: he is in Africa and South America and India. If we maintain our standard of living, individual and national, in spite of world penury, we shall be ashamed to face God.

You shall not bear false witness

It is said that Catholics, in comparison with Protestants, are poor in the practice of virtues such as honesty, uprightness and integrity. There is not enough collected evidence to justify a generalisation: but this is true, that if Catholics are known as untruthful and shifty in ordinary matters they do not gain credence for the divine truth committed to them.

Truthfulness is much more than not telling lies. There are truths the very possession of which brings a duty to pass them on. If we saw someone about to drink poison by mistake we should be bound to say what we know: his health and life would be our responsibility. The truths we have by revelation were committed by Christ to the Church in trust for mankind, who need them for their happiness. The Church has to pass them on, and we are the Church as well as the Pope and the Bishops. The ministry of the word is more than ever today a layman's task, because he has the ear of millions who will never hear a Bishop in their lives. 'Faith comes by hearing, but hearing the Word of Christ' (Rom 10:17). Christians should 'always have your answer ready for people who ask you the reason for the hope that you all have' (1 Pet 3:15).

The first duty – and it is serious – is to know the Word of God. If the whole range of Christian doctrine, scripture and tradition is too much to face, the job of knowing can be tackled from the needs of those one meets or is likely to meet. What are the non-Catholic Christian, the communist, atheist and agnostic objections to Christianity in general and Catholic Christianity in particular? What is their version of the truth, and where is it erroneous? No Catholic in English-speaking countries can go very far without being challenged. Educated Catholics should be ashamed if they are unable to defend the truths they profess, to state them intelligently and to meet a second and third assault. They cannot hope to convince those unwilling to accept Christian truth, but at least he can show he is reasonable in staying where he is. Learning for his own satisfaction is not enough. He must be able to express truth in the language of his hearers. Otherwise he is a blind guide, or an informant talking in double-dutch. Too often Catholics when asked for explanations or information have to answer 'Sorry! I'm a stranger here myself', or use a gibberish which confirms the questioner in his opinion that Catholicism is indeed a foreign religion.

Part of the truth is to know the other side, its doctrines and history, not necessarily as a specialist but in a measure sufficient for effective communication. That is particularly necessary for serious efforts towards unity in a country like England with a great variety of Protestant sects. It is no more than courtesy to know one's guests and companions.

More important than apologetics is the presentation of Christianity as the answer to man's desire for happiness.

We say that our religion makes life worth living. People whose present life is not worth living look for an alternative to despair and cynicism. We have it: we should be able to show it in its attractiveness. Given a firm conviction, we still need to train ourselves to put what we know into understandable and appealing words. (If we can't express what we know it is doubtful that we know it).

That is a strenuous programme. It would be easy to reject it, but it will not be so easy to explain the rejection to Our Lord when He asks about the spiritual works of mercy.

There is, finally, the need to bear witness to the truth in deed. Words need the backing of a way of life: they have to be recommended by the goodness of charity, uprightness, justice, dependability. It is when we are accepted as honourable persons that we are listened to when speaking the Word of God.

Informative Catholic Reading

We hope that you have enjoyed reading this booklet.

If you would like to find out more about CTS booklets - we'll send you our free information pack and catalogue.

Please send us your details:

Name ....

Address ....

....

....

Postcode ....

Telephone..

Email ....

Send to: CTS, 40-46 Harleyford Road,
              Vauxhall, London
              SE11 5AY

Tel: 020 7640 0042
Fax: 020 7640 0046
Email: info@cts-online.org.uk